Jell-O Salad Recipes

by Ann Sullivan

Published in USA by:

Ann Sullivan
217 N. Seacrest Blvd #9
Boynton Beach
FL 33425

© Copyright 2017

ISBN-13: 978-1548463847
ISBN-10: 1548463841

Table of Contents

Cranberry Fruit JELL-O Salad

Ingredients

- 1 (8 oz.) can crushed pineapple, drained, juice reserved

- 1/2 c. Ocean Spray® Cranberry Juice Cocktail

- 2 tbsps. lemon juice

- 1 (3 oz.) package raspberry flavored gelatin

- 1 (16 oz.) can Ocean Spray® Whole Berry Cranberry Sauce

- 1/2 c. celery, chopped

Directions

Combine all juices in a saucepan and bring to a boil. Remove from burner and add gelatin stirring until it is dissolved. Take the fork and break the cranberry sauce up into pieces. Slip sauce into the gelatin mixture. Stick in the refrigerator until set. Add remaining ingredients and pour into 4-c. mold. Continue to chill until it becomes firm.

Lemon Lime JELL-O Salad

Ingredients

- 1 (3 oz.) package lemon flavored gelatin mix

- 1 (3 oz.) package lime flavored gelatin mix

- 4 c. boiling water

- 1 tbsp. apple cider vinegar

- 2 stalks celery, finely chopped

- 1/2 c. chopped pimento-stuffed green olives

- 2 carrots, peeled and grated

Directions

Stir both lemon and lime mixes in large bowl. Add bowling water and stir until mixture has dissolved fully. Add vinegar and cover placing in the refrigerator for at least one hour until it thickens. Stir in remaining ingredients when gelatin is thickened being careful not to let it get too hard. Pour into 1 quart mold and refrigerate around 3 hours. Serve unmolded on a plate.

Congealed Chicken JELL-O Salad

Ingredients

- 1 (4 lb.) whole chicken

- 1/2 c. chopped sweet pickle

- 1 c. mayonnaise

- 1 (8 oz.) package cream cheese

- 1 (10.75 oz.) can condensed cream of mushroom soup

- 2 (.25 oz.) envelopes unflavored gelatin

Directions

Boil the chicken, drain, then cool. Chop the meat up in pieces and mix with the pickles and mayo in bowl. Heat mushroom soup and plain gelatin in a saucepan until the gelatin dissolves, then take off heat and add the cream cheese to stir. Mix the chicken mixture with the soup mixture and smooth out then pour into mold and chill.

Grandma's Cranberry-Orange JELL-O Salad

Ingredients

- 1 (6 oz.) package raspberry flavored gelatin mix

- 2 c. boiling water

- 1 (16 oz.) can whole berry cranberry sauce

- 1 (8 oz.) can crushed pineapple, un-drained

- 1 c. chopped celery

- 1 c. chopped pecans

- 1 tsp. orange zest

- 1 (4 oz.) package cream cheese, softened

- 1/2 c. whipped topping, or amount to taste

Directions

Pour the gelatin mix in a bowl and dissolve with the boiling water as directed. Add the cranberry sauce, pineapple, celery, pecans, and orange zest. Mix well then put in mold and chill for 8 hours. Make the topping mixture by beating the cream cheese together with half of whipped topping. When this is smooth, add the remaining topping until desired consistency and un-mold previous mixture and top it with the whipped cream cheese mixture, spreading it on top.

Holiday JELL-O Salad

Ingredients

- 1 c. crushed pineapple, drained with juice reserved

- 1 c. water, or as needed

- 1 (3 oz.) package lime flavored gelatin mix

- 1 (3 oz.) package lemon flavored gelatin mix

- 1 c. mayonnaise

- 1 c. canned evaporated milk

- 1 c. small curd cottage cheese

- 1/2 c. coarsely chopped pecans

Directions

Mix the drained pineapple juice with enough water to yield 2 c. and pour in a pot and boil. Combine both gel mixes and set aside. Mix the mayo and evaporated milk in a bowl. Add the gelatin mixes and blend the pineapple, cottage cheese, and pecans together. Put it all in a serving dish and chill 4 hours or overnight.

Cranberry JELL-O Salad

Ingredients

- 2 (3 oz.) packages cherry flavored gelatin mix
- 1 (16 oz.) can whole cranberry sauce
- 1 (20 oz.) can crushed pineapple with juice
- 1 (8 oz.) package cream cheese
- 1 c. chopped pecans
- 1 tbsp. mayonnaise

Directions

Reserve ¼ c. of the pineapple juice after draining. Dissolve gelatin mix in 2 c. hot water and add the pineapple and cranberries. Take ½ of gelatin fruit mixture and chill until solid. Combine mayo, cream cheese, ¼ c. pineapple juice and pecans and spread over the firm gelatin. Chill for 10 minutes. Spread room temperature gelatin over chilled cream cheese mixture and return to refrigerator to set.

Cucumber JELL-O Salad

Ingredients

- 2 (3 oz.) packages lime flavored gelatin mix
- 2 c. boiling water
- 1 (8 oz.) package cream cheese, softened
- 1 c. Miracle Whip
- 1 medium cucumber, peeled and chopped
- 1 dill pickle
- 1 tbsp. grated onion

Directions

Mix gelatin mix and boiling water in bowl and stir, set aside. Put all other ingredients in a blender on high until creamy. Add into the gelatin mixture and put in mold and chill 3 hours.

Buttermilk JELL-O Salad

Ingredients

- 1 (20 oz.) can crushed pineapple, with juice
- 1 (6 oz.) package apricot or peach flavored gelatin mix
- 2 c. buttermilk
- 1 (8 oz.) container frozen whipped topping, thawed

Directions

Put the pineapple and juice in a medium saucepan, and bring to a boil. Add the gelatin mix and stir until dissolved. Take out and place in a bowl, chilling until almost set, (1 hour). Stir in buttermilk, and chill again until thickened. Folding in whipped topping, and refrigerate until firm, at least 4 hours.

JELL-O Carrot Salad

Ingredients

- 1 (6 oz.) package lemon flavored gelatin mix
- 1 (20 oz.) can crushed pineapple, drained with juice reserved
- 4 large carrots, shredded

Directions

Use the instructions on the lemon Jell-O box, add the pineapple juice instead of water. Chill in the refrigerator for one hour until it thickens. Stir in uncrushed pineapples and carrots, then refrigerate again until set.

Orange Sherbet JELL-O Salad

Ingredients

- 2 (6 oz.) packages orange flavored gelatin
- 4 c. boiling water
- 1 quart orange sherbet
- 2 (11 oz.) cans mandarin oranges
- 3 bananas, sliced

Directions

Prepare Jell-O as directed and stir in fruit & sherbet, mix together well. Pour into a 9x13 dish and chill until set. Serve cold. Place the mixture in 9x13 inch dish and chill in the fridge until set (4 hours)

Molded Cucumber JELL-O Salad

Ingredients

- 1 large cucumber, peeled and shredded
- 1 (3 oz.) package lime flavored gelatin mix
- 1 1/4 c. boiling water
- 1 tbsp. white sugar
- 1 pinch salt
- 1 tbsp. white vinegar
- 1/2 c. mayonnaise

Directions

Shred the cucumber and put in a colander. Prepare the gelatin mix according to box and add the sugar, vinegar, and salt. Cool for 1 hour. When mix thickens, add mayo and cucumber then put into mold and chill 3 hrs.

Orange JELL-O Salad

Ingredients

- 1 (6 oz.) package orange flavored gelatin mix
- 1 c. boiling water
- 1 (3 oz.) package Neufchatel cheese, softened
- 1/4 c. low-fat mayonnaise
- 1 tbsp. apple cider vinegar
- 1 medium carrot, peeled and grated
- 1 (8 oz.) can crushed pineapple, with juice
- 1 c. fruit cocktail, drained

Directions

Prepare Jell-O as directed and add Neufchatel cheese and mayo, blending well. Cool gelatin mixture slightly. And add the remaining ingredients to put into mold. Cover and chill about 4 hours. Serve when set.

JELL-O Salad with Cranberry and Black Cherry

Ingredients

- 1 (6 oz.) package black cherry flavored gelatin mix

- 1 (16 oz.) container sour cream, room temperature

- 1 (16 oz.) can whole cranberry sauce

- 1 c. chopped walnuts

- 2 c. hot water

Directions

Stir cranberries in jell mix after mix has dissolved in hot water. Add sour cream and stir. Chill in fridge until almost set then add walnuts and chill for 4 hrs.

Marshmallow JELL-O Salad

Ingredients

- 7 fluid oz. lemon-lime flavored carbonated beverage

- 2 c. miniature marshmallows

- 1 (3 oz.) package lime flavored gelatin mix

- 8 oz. cream cheese

- 1 (20 oz.) can crushed pineapple with juice

- 3/4 c. chopped pecans

- 1 tsp. mayonnaise

- 1 c. frozen whipped topping, thawed

Directions

Combine soda and marshmallows and stir over medium heat until marshmallows melt. Remove from the heat to cool. Dissolve the gelatin in the cream cheese. Stir in the pineapple and juice, pecans, mayo and whipped topping. Mix and pour into a 7x11 dish to chill in fridge.

Cranberry JELL-O Salad

Ingredients

- 2 (3 oz.) packages raspberry flavored gelatin mix

- 1 c. white sugar

- 2 c. boiling water

- 1 1/2 c. cold water

- 1 lb. cranberries

- 1 orange

- 1 1/2 c. crushed pineapple, drained

- 2 c. seedless red grapes, halved

- 1 1/2 c. diced apples

Directions

Combine gelatin mix, sugar, and boiling water and stir until it dissolves. Pour pineapple juice and cold water in and chill until it thickens. Blend orange and cranberries in blender on high for 1 or 2 minutes and add remaining fruit to the cranberry mixture. Put in a 9x13 pan and chill overnight.

Blueberry JELL-O Salad

Ingredients

- 3 (6 oz.) packages raspberry flavored gelatin mix
- 3 1/4 c. boiling water
- 1 (.25 oz.) package unflavored gelatin
- 1/2 c. cold water
- 1 c. half-and-half
- 1 c. white sugar
- 1 tsp. vanilla extract
- 1 (8 oz.) package cream cheese, softened
- 1 c. boiling water
- 1 (21 oz.) can blueberry pie filling

Directions

Dissolve flavored gelatin in boiling water and pour in 9x13 pan and chill 1 hour. Mix cold water and unflavored gelatin in medium pan and add, sugar, half 'n half and vanilla and cook on medium heat, stirring constantly. Remove to cool.

Applesauce JELL-O Salad

Ingredients

- 2 c. water
- 1/2 c. cinnamon red hot candies
- 1 (6 oz.) package cherry flavored gelatin mix
- 2 c. applesauce

Directions

Dissolve ½ c. hot candies in the boiling water and add gelatin. Put in small bowl and stir in the applesauce. Chill for hours.

Lime JELL-O Salad

Ingredients

- 1 c. boiling water
- 1 (6 oz.) package lime flavored gelatin mix
- 1 (20 oz.) can crushed pineapple, drained with juice reserved
- 1 (8 oz.) package cream cheese, softened
- 2 c. heavy cream
- 1 c. chopped pecans

Directions

Mix Jell-O as directed and add ½ c. pineapple juice. Chill until thickened 1 hour. Bring pineapple and juice to a boil in saucepan. Cover and simmer 5 minutes then remove to cool. Mix remaining ingredients and chilled juice mixture in medium bowl then pour in bowl to serve. Chill until set or 4 hours.

Lime JELL-O Salad with Cabbage

Ingredients

- 1 (6 oz.) package lime flavored gelatin mix
- 3/4 c. boiling water
- 1/4 tsp. salt
- 3/4 c. cold water
- 1 c. shredded cabbage
- 1/2 c. grated carrots
- 1/2 c. chopped walnuts

Directions

Prepare gelatin as directed and stir in the salt & cold water. Chill till it thickens. Add remaining ingredients and put in 8-inch greased mold. Chill 4 hours. Serve.

Cranberry Nut JELL-O Salad

Ingredients

- 1 (6 oz.) package black cherry flavored gelatin mix
- 1 (16 oz.) container sour cream, room temperature
- 1 (16 oz.) can whole cranberry sauce
- 1 c. chopped walnuts
- 2 c. hot water

Directions

Prepare gelatin as directed on box then stir in cranberries & sour cream, mix well and chill for 1 hour.

Festive JELL-O Salad

Ingredients

- 1 (3 oz.) package orange flavored gelatin mix

- 1 (16 oz.) container cottage cheese

- 1 (8 oz.) tub frozen whipped topping, thawed

- 1 (10 oz.) can mandarin oranges, drained and halved

- 1 (8 oz.) can pineapple tidbits, drained

- 1/2 (4 oz.) jar maraschino cherries, drained and halved

- 1/3 c. chopped pecans (optional)

Directions

Mix cottage cheese and orange gelatin in bowl until well mixed. Add whipped topping, pecans and various fruits. Put in greased mold and chill 2 hours.

Mama's Cranberry JELL-O Salad

Ingredients

- 1 (3 oz.) package strawberry flavored gelatin mix
- 1 c. boiling water
- 3/4 c. cold water
- 2 oranges - peeled, sectioned, and cut into bite-size pieces
- 1 lemon - peeled, seeded and chopped
- 3 medium tart apples, peeled and chopped
- 2 c. cranberries, coarsely chopped
- 1/4 c. white sugar, or to taste

Directions

Prepare gelatin as directed and add the cold water and stir. Pour in to a mold and chill 1 hour. Add the fruit to bowl sprinkling the sugar on top of fruit. Leave out for fruit to bleed. When gelatin is almost set, add the sugary fruit and chill 2 hours before serving.

Orange Tapioca JELL-O Salad

Ingredients

- 3 c. water

- 1 (3 oz.) package orange flavored gelatin mix

- 1 (3.4 oz.) package instant vanilla pudding mix

- 1 (3 oz.) package instant tapioca pudding mix

- 1 (15 oz.) can mandarin oranges, drained

- 1 (8 oz.) can crushed pineapple, drained

- 1 (8 oz.) tub frozen whipped topping, thawed

Directions

Combine all mixes in large pot with water and bring to a boil. Stir, then remove to cool completely. Add the fruit and cool whip and stir, putting in serving bowl. Chill 2 hours then fluff top with a spoon before serving to your hungry guests.

Raspberry Cinnamon JELL-O Salad

Ingredients

- 1 (3 oz.) package raspberry flavored gelatin mix
- 1 c. boiling water
- 1 (2.25 oz.) package cinnamon red hot candies
- 1 c. applesauce

Directions

Prepare gelatin and add hot candies to water until they melt. Mix in the applesauce and chill 3 hours.

Blueberry Pineapple JELL-O Salad

Ingredients

- 2 (3 oz.) packages grape flavored gelatin mix

- 2 c. boiling water

- 1 (8 oz.) can crushed pineapple, un-drained

- 1 (21 oz.) can blueberry pie filling

- Topping:

- 1 (8 oz.) package cream cheese, softened

- 1 c. sour cream

- 1/2 c. white sugar

- 1 tsp. vanilla extract

Directions

Prepare gelatin mix as directed with pineapple and pie filling. Add to glass dish or mold and chill 2 hours. Combine remaining ingredients and mix until creamy. Add to top of chilled mixture, then chill 2 hours.

Blueberry Lime JELL-O Salad

Ingredients

- 1 (3 oz.) package lime flavored gelatin mix
- 1 tbsp. sugar
- 2 tbsps. lime juice
- 1 1/2 c. boiling water
- 1 (8 oz.) container frozen whipped topping, thawed
- 1 pint fresh blueberries

Directions

Combine lime juice, sugar, gelatin, mix and boiling water in a medium bowl for 1 minute. Cover and chill 1 hour. Remove from fridge and whip until light in color. Add the whipped topping and blueberries. Chill for 4 hours in mold or serving dish.

Rhubarb JELL-O Salad

Ingredients

- 3 c. chopped fresh rhubarb
- 1/2 c. white sugar, or to taste
- 2 tbsps. water
- 1 (3 oz.) package raspberry flavored gelatin mix
- 1 c. cold water
- 1 c. chopped apple
- 1/2 c. chopped walnuts

Directions

Put sugar, rhubarb, and 2 Tbsp. water over medium heat in saucepan and boil for 15 minutes.
Stir to make a sauce and reserve 1 c. Stir reserved c. with raspberry gelatin until it dissolves. Add cold water, walnuts and apples. Chill in dish 2-4 hours.

Horseradish and Pineapple JELL-O Salad

Ingredients

- 1 c. boiling water

- 1/2 tbsp. unflavored gelatin

- 1 (3 oz.) package lime flavored gelatin mix

- 1 c. mayonnaise

- 1 c. small curd cottage cheese

- 2 tsps. prepared horseradish

- 1 (20 oz.) can crushed pineapple, drained

- 1 c. chopped pecans

- 1 pinch salt

Directions

Combine unflavored gelatin, lime mix & boiling water in medium bowl and stir until dissolved. Set aside for 1 hour to cool. Mix together remaining ingredients except pecans, pineapple and salt in bowl and beat with electric mixer until foamy. Add the items left and mix by hand in bowl. Combine both mixtures in mold and chill until set, 2 hours.

JELL-O Salad with Avocado and Toasted Pecans

Ingredients

- 1 (6 oz.) package lime flavored gelatin mix
- 1 3/4 c. boiling water
- 1 (8 oz.) package cream cheese, softened
- 1/2 c. chopped celery
- 1 1/2 avocados, peeled and mashed
- 1/2 c. mayonnaise
- 1/2 tsp. salt
- 1 tsp. onion juice (optional)
- 6 butter lettuce leaves, rinsed
- 1/2 c. mayonnaise
- 1/4 c. confectioners' sugar, or to taste
- 1 tbsp. lemon juice, or to taste
- 1/2 c. pecan halves, toasted

Directions

Prepare gelatin and set aside, then combine cream cheese, celery, avocado, mayo & salt in small bowl. Slowly add gelatin mixture and pour in 11 x 7-inch glass dish and chill 2 hours. Make the topping with the mayo, lemon juice and confectioners' sugar in bowl and stir, mixing well then drizzling over the gelatin. Cut into squares and serve on top of a leaf of butter lettuce and garnish with pecans.

Orange JELL-O Buttermilk Salad

Ingredients

- 1 (20 oz.) can crushed pineapple, un-drained
- 3 tbsps. white sugar
- 1 (6 oz.) package orange flavored gelatin
- 2 c. buttermilk
- 1 (8 oz.) container frozen whipped topping, thawed

Directions

Bring pineapple and juice to a boil while stirring, add the sugar and dissolve the gelatin. Remove from heat to cool. Add the buttermilk and return to fridge for 1 hour. Whip in the topping and pour mixture into a greased mold. Chill overnight.

Persimmon Pulp JELL-O Salad

Ingredients

- 1 (6 oz.) package orange flavored gelatin mix
- 1 1/4 c. grapefruit juice
- 1 c. mandarin oranges, drained and quartered
- 2 c. persimmon pulp

Directions

Boil grapefruit juice in small saucepan, then combine it with gelatin mix in a small bowl to chill for 90 minutes. Combine mandarin oranges and persimmon pulp with chilled mixture and return to refrigerator for 3 hours. Cut into squares to serve.

Orange JELL-O Salad

Ingredients

- 1 egg, beaten
- 3/4 c. white sugar
- 1/3 c. all-purpose flour
- 1 (15 oz.) can pineapple chunks, drained
- 1 tbsp. margarine, softened
- 1 tsp. vanilla extract
- 1 (8 oz.) container frozen whipped topping, thawed
- 1 (3 oz.) package orange flavored gelatin mix
- 1 c. boiling water
- 1 c. water
- 4 bananas, sliced

Directions

Mix egg, flour, sugar, pineapple chunks, vanilla, and margarine in a saucepan. Cook until mixture thickens.

Add to an 8x8 dish. Blend in the cool whip and chill for over an hour.
Prepare gelatin mix as directed, adding remaining water, then chill until thick. Blend pineapple and bananas in gelatin mixture and spread on top of other mix. Chill for 3 hours.

Seven Layer JELL-O Salad

Ingredients

- 7 (3 oz.) packages assorted fruit flavored gelatin mix

- 4 1/2 c. boiling water, divided

- 4 1/2 c. cold water, divided

- 1 (12 fluid oz.) can evaporated milk, divided

- 1 (8 oz.) container frozen whipped topping, thawed

Directions

Spray a 9x13 inch dish with nonstick spray. Prepare Jell-O as directed and add ¾ c. of cold water, chill for 45 minutes. Dissolve 1 more package of gelatin in ½ c. of boiling water. Add ½ c. cold water and ½ c. evaporated milk. Spread over fist layer and chill for 45 minutes. Repeat until all gelatin is gone, then top with cool whip.

Raspberry Cherry JELL-O Salad

Ingredients

- 1 (16 oz.) package cottage cheese

- 1 (8 oz.) container frozen whipped topping, thawed

- 1 (15 oz.) can crushed pineapple, drained

- 1 (12 oz.) can cherry pie filling

- 1 (3 oz.) package raspberry flavored gelatin mix

Directions

Combine all ingredients in a large bowl and pour gelatin mix over mixture to mix well. Then put into separate bowls and chill for 3 to 4 hours.

Lemon-Lime JELL-O Salad

Ingredients

- 1 (3 oz.) package lime flavored gelatin mix
- 1 tsp. white sugar
- 1 c. boiling water
- 1 (8 oz.) package cream cheese
- 1 (8 oz.) can crushed pineapple, with juice
- 1 tsp. vanilla extract
- 1 c. lemon-lime flavored carbonated beverage
- 1/2 c. chopped pecans

Directions

Dissolve lime mix and sugar in hot water, and add cream cheese. Blend well until it melts into smaller chunks. Add soda, nuts, pineapple, and juice. Chill overnight.

Creamy Cranberry JELL-O Salad

Ingredients

- 1 (12 oz.) package fresh cranberries

- 1 c. white sugar

- 1 (6 oz.) package red gelatin mix

- 1 (8 oz.) can crushed pineapple, drained

- 3/4 c. orange juice

- 1 apple with peel, grated

- 1 c. chopped pecans

- 1 c. whipping cream

- 1 (8 oz.) package cream cheese, softened

Directions

Blend cranberries in a blender and dissolve sugar over top by stirring. Boil ¾ c. water and add red gelatin mix, and then let cool. Pour the mix over the cranberries, adding fruit juices, apple, and pecans. Stir well. Cover and chill for 8 hours. Fold cream cheese in with whipping cream. Layer half of the cranberry mixture into serving bowls, and then top with the cream mixture. Repeat with the remaining cranberry mixture. Serve chilled.

Apple Cinnamon JELL-O Salad

Ingredients

- 1/3 c. cinnamon red hot candies

- 1 1/2 c. boiling water

- 1 (3 oz.) package lemon flavored gelatin mix

- 1 1/2 c. applesauce

Directions

Boil 1 ½ c. water and dissolve the hot candies. Then, add lemon gelatin and stir. Pour in apple sauce, adding ice cubes to cool. Place in refrigerator for 3 hours. Serve with whipped cream on top.

Pineapple JELL-O Salad

Ingredients

- 1 (3 oz.) package lemon flavored gelatin mix
- 1 (3 oz.) package lime flavored gelatin mix
- 2 c. boiling water
- 2 c. water
- 1 (15 oz.) can crushed pineapple, with juice
- 1 (16 oz.) package small curd cottage cheese
- 3 tbsps. prepared horseradish
- 1 c. mayonnaise
- 1 c. chopped pecans

Directions

Prepare the gelatin mix as directed, and combine both lemon and lime with boiling water. Chill for about 1 hour, or until it is set. Take out of fridge and mix in the remaining ingredients. Chill again for 3 hours.

Thanksgiving JELL-O Salad

Ingredients

- 2 c. water

- 1 (6 oz.) package strawberry flavored gelatin mix

- 1 (10 oz.) package frozen strawberries, thawed

- 1 (16 oz.) can whole cranberry sauce

- 1/2 c. chopped pecans

- 8 leaves lettuce

- 1 (3 oz.) package cream cheese, softened

- 1 c. sour cream

- 1/3 c. white sugar

- 1 tbsp. lemon juice

Directions

Prepare Jell-O mix as directed, and stir in cranberry sauce, strawberries, and pecans. Then, transfer to a mold. Chill overnight. Surround the base of the serving plate with lettuce leaves, and put mold on top. Blend together the remaining ingredients for the topping with electric mixer. Blend well. Top with cream cheese mixture and serve with lettuce.

Fall JELO Salad

Ingredients

- 1 (20 oz.) can crushed pineapple with juice

- 2/3 c. white sugar

- 1 (3 oz.) package lemon flavored gelatin mix

- 1 (8 oz.) package cream cheese, softened

- 1 c. diced, unpeeled apples

- 1 c. chopped nuts

- 1 c. chopped celery

- 1 c. frozen whipped topping, thawed

Directions

Boil pineapple juice and sugar in a medium saucepan for about 3 minutes. Stir in the lemon mix and dissolve. Add the cream cheese. Remove to cool for 10 to 15 minutes. Stir together the apples, nuts, topping, and celery to mix well. Put mix in a square pan and chill for 4 hours.

Pineapple Coconut JELL-O Salad

Ingredients

- 1 (3 oz.) package lemon flavored gelatin mix
- 1 (3 oz.) package orange flavored gelatin mix
- 2 c. boiling water
- 1 (20 oz.) can crushed pineapple, drained
- 1 (16 oz.) package miniature marshmallows
- 2 c. pineapple juice
- 1 c. white sugar
- 2 eggs, lightly beaten
- 5 tbsps. all-purpose flour
- 3 bananas, sliced
- 1 tbsp. lemon juice
- 2 (1...3 oz.) envelopes whipped topping mix
- 1 (8 oz.) package cream cheese, softened
- 1 c. shredded coconut, toasted

Directions

Prepare Jell-O as directed and add drained pineapple and marshmallows to both the lemon and orange mixes. Chill till firm. In a medium saucepan, mix pineapple juice, sugar, eggs, and flour and cook until it becomes thick. Stir and then remove from the heat to cool, and top over the gelatin mix. Squeeze lemon juice over sliced bananas, and then drain fruit and add to gelatin mixture as another layer. Prepare topping mix like the directions say, and fold in cream cheese. Layer over bananas, putting coconut on the very top. Chill for a few hours before serving.

Orange Pineapple Nut JELL-O Salad

Ingredients

- 2 1/2 c. crushed pineapple, with juice
- 1 (3 oz.) package orange flavored gelatin
- 1 (3 oz.) package cream cheese, softened
- 1 c. chopped pimento
- 1 c. heavy cream, whipped
- 1 c. diced celery
- 1 c. chopped walnuts

Directions

Boil pineapple and juice on medium heat and dissolve gelatin. Remove to cool in the refrigerator until almost set. Stir the chopped pimento into the cream cheese and blend well. Add the gelatin mixture with cream cheese mixture and then blend in the whipped cream, nuts, and celery. Transfer to a 1 ½ quart mold, chill until firm.

Strawberry Pretzel JELL-O Salad

Ingredients

- 2 c. crushed pretzels

- 3/4 c. margarine, melted

- 2 tsps. white sugar

- 1 (8 oz.) package cream cheese

- 3/4 c. white sugar

- 4 1/2 oz. frozen whipped topping, thawed

- 1 (6 oz.) package strawberry flavored gelatin

- 2 c. boiling water

- 2 (10 oz.) packages frozen strawberries

Directions

Preheat oven to 400 degrees. Mix together margarine, pretzels, and sugar in a bowl, and then transfer to a 9x13 inch baking dish. Cook for 8 minutes, and then cool. Combine cream cheese, sugar, and whipped topping. After the pretzels cool, pour over mix. Dissolve strawberry Jell-O, as directed, in a bowl, and add strawberries. Cool for 15 minutes. Put the strawberry mixture over the cream cheese mixture, and chill for 4 hours.

Blueberry Sour Cream JELL-O Mold

Ingredients

- 2 c. boiling water

- 1 (6 oz.) package raspberry flavored gelatin mix

- 1 (15 oz.) can blueberries

- 1 (8 oz.) can crushed pineapple

- 1 (8 oz.) package cream cheese, softened

- 1/2-pint sour cream

- 3 tbsps. white sugar

- 2 tsps. vanilla extract

- 1/4 c. chopped pecans

Directions

Dissolve the raspberry Jell-O, as directed, and stir in the blueberries and pineapple. Transfer to a 2-quart mold and chill for 2 hours. Mix together all other ingredients, excluding pecans, and blend well. Pour over raspberry mixture once set. Add pecans to the top. Chill once more before serving.

Raspberry JELL-O Mold

Ingredients

- 1 (10 oz.) package frozen raspberries - thawed and drained, juice reserved

- 1 c. water

- 12 oz. cranberries

- 1/2 c. white sugar

- 2 (3 oz.) packages raspberry flavored gelatin mix

Directions

Bring cranberries, sugar, raspberry juice, and 1 c. of water to boil in a saucepan, and stir until the skins on the cranberries burst. Remove to cool. Add Jell-O and stir in the raspberries. Transfer to a 2-quart mold. Chill until firm.

Strawberry Delight JELL-O Salad

Ingredients

- 1 (16 oz.) container frozen whipped topping, thawed

- 1 (6 oz.) package strawberry flavored gelatin

- 3 (15...25 oz.) cans fruit cocktail, drained

- 1 (11 oz.) can mandarin oranges, drained

- 2 c. grapes

- 2 c. miniature marshmallows

Directions

Combine all ingredients in a large bowl, and mix well. Chill and stir before serving.

Whipped Lime JELL-O Salad

Ingredients

- 1 (3 oz.) package lime flavored gelatin mix
- 1 c. boiling water
- 1 c. cold evaporated milk
- 1 (12 oz.) package vanilla wafers, crushed

Directions

Prepare Jell-O as directed and chill for 1 hour. Chill a bowl and beater to use to whip the evaporated milk together so that it is thick like cool whip. Stir into the gelatin. Cover the mixture and chill overnight. Toss cookie crumbs on top of unmolded gelatin serve.

Lemon Pear JELL-O Salad

Ingredients

- 1 (15 oz.) can pear halves

- 1 (3 oz.) package lemon flavored gelatin

- 1 (8 oz.) package cream cheese

- 1/2 c. chopped pecans

- 2 c. frozen whipped topping, thawed

Directions

Add water to pear syrup to equal 1 c. Stir gelatin in a saucepan with syrup, and bring to a boil to dissolve. Cool until set. Combine all other ingredients until smooth, and transfer to a mold or bowl. Chill for 3 hours.

Pineapple Cranberry JELL-O Salad

Ingredients

- 2 (3 oz.) packages raspberry flavored gelatin mix
- 1 (16 oz.) can whole cranberry sauce
- 1/2 tsp. orange zest
- 1/3 c. orange juice
- 2 tbsps. lemon juice
- 1 (20 oz.) can pineapple tidbits, drained
- 3/4 c. sliced celery

Directions

Dissolve Jell-O mix as directed, adding pineapple juice. Bring to a boil. Remove to cool. Combine all remaining ingredients and blend until thick. Transfer to a mold or 8-inch pan, and chill until firm.

Apricot Orange JELL-O Salad

Ingredients

- 1 (15 oz.) can apricot halves, drained with juice reserved

- 2 (8 oz.) cans crushed pineapple, drained with juice reserved

- 2 (6 oz.) packages orange flavored gelatin mix

- 2 c. hot water

- 1/2 c. chopped walnuts

- 1 c. miniature marshmallows

- 1 c. white sugar

- 1 egg, beaten

- 3 tbsps. all-purpose flour

- 2 tbsps. butter

- 1 c. heavy cream

- 1/2 c. shredded Colby longhorn cheese

Directions

Reserve the pineapple and apricot syrup adding water if needed to equal 2 ½ c. Combine dissolved gelatin and reserved 1 ½ c. fruit syrup and then set aside, cooling. Add the other fruits, nuts, and marshmallows to Jell-O mixture and stir well. Grease a 9x13 inch pan and transfer to chill until firm. Heat the flour, sugar, egg, remaining fruit syrup, and butter in a sauce pan, stir so it doesn't scold. Let chill. Blend whip cream and fold into the custard mixture. Pour on top of gelatin and chill in the refrigerator. Top with cheese before you serve.

Spicy Peach JELL-O Salad

Ingredients

- 1 (1 lb.) can peach, sliced
- 1/4 c. vinegar
- 1/2 c. sugar
- 12 whole cloves
- 1/8 tsp. cinnamon
- 1 (3 oz.) package peach Jell-O
- 3/4 c. water, cold

Directions

Drain the peaches, and reserve ¾ c. of syrup. Chop up the peaches and boil vinegar, syrup, and spices slowly. Simmer for 10 minutes, adding peaches. Discard the cloves and strain syrup, adding peach juice to yield 1 c. Add Jell-O to hot syrup, dissolve and then add cold water and sliced peaches. Chill, then transfer to the mold.

Strawberry Pineapple Jell-O Salad

Ingredients

- 1 (3 oz.) box strawberry gelatin
- 1 c. boiling water
- 3 bananas, mashed
- 1 (20 oz.) can crushed pineapple
- 30 oz. frozen strawberries, un-drain
- 1 (1 pint) container sour cream

Directions

Prepare Jell-O as directed and combine it with bananas, un-drained frozen strawberries, and pineapple. Take half of the mixture, and put it into a pan to chill for 45 minutes. Add the sour cream to the top. Take the remaining half of mixture and combine it to chill. Then cut into triangles.

Crunchy Strawberry Jell-O Salad

Ingredients

- 2 c. crushed pretzels

- 1/2-1 c. melted butter

- 3 tbsps. sugar

- 1 (2 oz.) package Dream Whip (prepare as directed on package)

- 1 (8 oz.) package cream cheese, softened

- 3/4 c. sugar

- 1 (3 oz.) package strawberry Jell-O gelatin dessert (prepared as directed on package)

- 1 (12-16 oz.) package frozen strawberries, thawed

Directions

Preheat oven to 350 degrees. Combine sugar, pretzels, and melted butter in a bowl. Press into a 13x9 inch pan and bake for 10 minutes. Stir together Dream whip, cream cheese, and ¾ c. sugar. Add the pretzel mixture. Cool in the refrigerator. Put prepared Jell-O over cream cheese mixture, adding the strawberries. Chill until completely satisfied with the consistency. Cut into triangles.

Three Layer Orange Jell-O Salad

Ingredients

- 1 package orange Jell-O

- 1 can crushed pineapple, drained, save juice

- 1 (8 oz.) package cream cheese

- 1 container Cool Whip

- 3/4 c. sugar

- 2 tbsps. flour

- 2 eggs, well beaten

- 1 tsp. lemon juice

- 1 c. pineapple juice (use juice drained from pineapple and add water to measure 1 c.)

Directions

Prepare Jell-O as directed, minus ¼ c. water. Add the crushed pineapple. Transfer to a 9x13 inch glass rectangular pan. Chill. Fold the cool whip and cream cheese together to pour over Jell-O. Cool again in the refrigerator. After you blend the flour and sugar, add the pineapple juice and lemon juice and cook until thickened. Pour over the cool whip layer and chill in the fridge again before serving.

Ginger Ale and Peach Jell-O Salad

Ingredients

- 1 (4 oz.) package orange flavor gelatin

- 1 c. boiling water

- 1 c. ginger ale

- 2 c. sliced peaches

Directions

Dissolve Jell-O as directed and add ginger ale and peaches. Stir. Transfer to 8x8 inch pan and chill for 2 to 3 hours. Cut and serve.

Fruity Jell-O Salad

Ingredients

- 1 (4 oz.) package raspberry gelatin powder
- 1 (4 oz.) package berry blue gelatin mix
- 2 1/2 c. boiling water
- 1 c. crushed pineapple, packed in fruit juice, undrained
- 1/4 c. frozen unsweetened blueberries
- 1/4 c. frozen unsweetened raspberry
- 1 c. diced banana

Directions

Prepare Jell-O as directed and add pineapple, frozen blueberries, and raspberries. Stir well and add bananas. Transfer to 8x8 pan. Chill for 3 hours, and cut into squares.

Berry Jell-O Salad

Ingredients

- 1 (6 oz.) package raspberry Jell-O gelatin or
  2 (3 oz.) packages raspberry Jell-O gelatin

- 1 (10 oz.) package frozen raspberries, thawed and
  drained thoroughly

- 1 (16 oz.) can whole berry cranberry sauce

- 1 (20 oz.) can crushed pineapple in juice, drained
  thoroughly

Directions

Drain fruit thoroughly and add prepared Jell-O mix. Use
the drained fruit juice for the cold water instead.
Combine with the remaining ingredients and mix well.
Transfer Into a 9x13 inch glass dish and chill over night
until set.

Cream Cheese Pretzel Jell-O Salad

Ingredients

- 2 c. crushed pretzels

- 3/4 c. melted butter

- 1/2 tsp. cinnamon

- 3 tbsps. sugar

- 8 oz. cream cheese, softened

- 8 oz. Cool Whip, thawed

- 1/4 c. sugar

- 1/2 tsp. vanilla

- 1 tbsp. grated fresh lemon rind

- 6 oz. berry gelatin

- 2 c. boiling water

- 2 (10 oz.) packages frozen berries (strawberries, blackberries, whatever sounds good to you!)

Directions

Crush the pretzels up and mix well with the sugar, cinnamon, and melted butter. Pour in a 9x13 inch pan and cook at 400 degrees for 8 minutes. Grate the lemon rind and mix with cool whip, sugar, and vanilla. Pour over cooled pretzel mixture. Prepare Jell-O as directed and add frozen fruit. Add to pan and chill until set.

Peach Jell-O Salad

Ingredients

- 1 package peach Jell-O

- 1 1/2 c. boiling water

- 1 (3 oz.) package cream cheese

- 3 tbsps. sugar

- 1 dash salt

- 1 tsp. vanilla

- 1 tsp. lemon juice

- 1 (8 oz.) can crushed pineapple

Directions

Prepare Jell-O as directed and add cream cheese. Stir in salt, sugar, vanilla, and lemon juice well.
Add pineapple and its juices. Chill to set.

7-Up Jell-O Salad

Ingredients

- 2 cans crushed pineapple, drained

- 1 (6 oz.) box lemon Jell-O gelatin

- 2 c. 7-Up soda

- 2 c. pineapple juice

- 4 tbsps. flour

- 4 tbsps. butter

- 2 eggs

- 2 c. whipped topping

Directions

Stir together Jell-O, 7-up, and pineapple, and then transfer to a 9x 13-inch dish. Chill to set. Bring all other ingredients to a boil in medium sauce pan and stir for 1 minute. Let cool. Mixed whipped topping with the cooled, cooked mixture and add to top of Jell-O.

Any Fruit Jell-O Salad

Ingredients

- 1 (6 oz.) package any flavor Jell-O gelatin

- 2 c. boiling water

- 1/2-3/4 c. plain yogurt or sour cream or cream cheese

- 12 ice cubes

- 3/4-1 1/2 c. any kind fruit, chopped (canned or fresh, except fresh pineapple)

Directions

Prepare Jell-O as directed, and then add the sour cream or cream cheese. Blend with an electric mixer. Take 12 ice cubes and add to mixture, remember to stir until they melt. Combine fruit and chill with mixture. Serve with baby marshmallow on top.

Apple Celery Jell-O Salad

Ingredients

- Orange Jell-O (Sugar Free works fine)
- Walnuts
- Apple
- Celery

Directions

Prepare Jell-O as directed on box, and add chopped walnuts. Add apple cubes and celery ribs to Jell-O. Transfer to mold. Chill for 3 hours. Serve.

Blueberry Cream Jell-O Salad

Ingredients

- 2 (3 oz.) packages grape Jell-O

- 2 c. boiling water

- 1 (8 oz.) can crushed pineapple, not drained

- 1 can blueberry pie filling

- Topping

- 8 oz. cream cheese (can use light or fat free)

- 1 c. sour cream (can use light or fat free)

- 1/2 c. sugar

- 1 tsp. vanilla

Directions

Prepare Jell-O, and add pie filling and pineapple. Chill until firm. When set, mix cream cheese, sugar, vanilla, and sour cream. Add to top of Jell-O.

Raspberry Whip Jell-O Salad

Ingredients

- 3 c. crushed pretzel sticks

- 3 tbsps. white sugar

- 3/4 c. margarine

- 2 c. Cool Whip

- 8 oz. cream cheese

- 1 c. white sugar

- 1 (1 large) box raspberry Jell-O gelatin

- 2 c. boiling water

- 2 (10 oz.) packages frozen raspberries (or blueberries, strawberries, blackberries)

Directions

Blend pretzels in a blender on pulse for 10 seconds. Add 3 tbsps. sugar and margarine. Pulse again to mix. Transfer to a 9x10 inch pan and cook for 10 minutes at 350 degrees.
Blend cream cheese, cool whip, and sugar in a blender. Add pretzels to the top. Chill. Prepare Jell-O as directed

and add frozen berries. Stir. Add to the top of cream cheese mixture and chill for 2 hours to set.

Orange Vanilla Jell-O Salad

Ingredients

- 2 (3 oz.) packages instant vanilla pudding

- 1 (3 oz.) package orange Jell-O

- 1 1/2 c. boiling water

- 1 (22 oz.) can mandarin oranges (with juice)

- 1 (16 oz.) container Cool Whip

Directions

Dissolve Jell-O as directed, and add pudding, oranges, and juice. Blend with cool whip, and serve.

Simple Jell-O Salad

Ingredients

- 1 (12 oz.) carton whipped topping
- 1 (3 oz.) package Jell-O gelatin, any flavor
- 1 (8 oz.) carton cottage cheese
- 1 (8 oz.) can crushed pineapple, drained

Directions

Transfer cool whip to a medium bowl and stir in Jell-O mix. Blend well. Add pineapples and cottage cheese. Chill till Jell-O set, and then serve.

Pineapple and Mandarin Orange Jell-O Salad

Ingredients

- 1 c. hot water
- 1 (6 oz.) package orange Jell-O
- 1 c. orange juice
- 1 c. sour cream
- 1 pint orange sherbet, slightly softened
- 1 c. pineapple tidbits, drained
- 1 (10 oz.) can mandarin orange segments, drained
- 1/4 c. maraschino cherry, drained and chopped
- 1/4 c. coconut, lightly toasted

Directions

Dissolve jell as directed, and add orange juice. Chill to thicken. Add sherbet and sour cream. Stir till foamy. Add desired fruit, and then transfer to a 2-quart mold. Chill overnight. Unmold and add coconut on top.

Luscious Jell-O Salad

Ingredients

- 2 packages strawberry Jell-O gelatin dessert
- 3 mashed bananas
- 1 c. boiling water
- 1 (10 oz.) package frozen strawberries
- 1 can crushed pineapple (drained)
- 1 pint sour cream

Directions

Combine prepared Jell-O with remaining ingredients, except the sour cream, in a bowl. Put ½ of the mixture in a 9x12 inch pan. Chill to set. Add sour cream to the top, and pour another half to top layer. Chill to set for 4 hours.

Orange Mallow Jell-O Salad

Ingredients

- 1 (3 oz.) box orange Jell-O

- 1 (8 oz.) package cream cheese

- 19 large marshmallows

- 1 c. milk

- 1 (15 oz.) can crushed pineapple

- 1 (11 oz.) can mandarin oranges

- 1/4 c. mayonnaise

- 1 (8 oz.) container Cool Whip

Directions

Blend the cream cheese and Jell-O. Dissolve
marshmallows with milk in a saucepan on medium heat.
Stir. Combine pineapple and oranges to Jell-O and
marshmallow mixture. Stir well. Blend with cool whip
and mayonnaise. Chill for 2 hours.

Jell-O Vegetable Salad

Ingredients

- 2 packages lime gelatin
- 1/2 c. finely diced red radish
- 1/2 c. finely diced green pepper
- 1/2 c. finely diced carrot
- Thousand Island dressing

Directions

Prepare Jell-O as directed, and let it set to thicken in the refrigerator. Add veggies, and chill again. Serve with Thousand Island dressing.

Frosted Jell-O Salad

Ingredients

- 2 (3 oz.) packages lemon Jell-O gelatin

- 2 c. boiling water

- 2 c. 7-Up soda

- 1 c. miniature marshmallow

- 1 c. crushed pineapple, drained (save juice)

- 2 large bananas, sliced

- 1/2 c. sugar

- 2 tbsps. flour

- 1 c. pineapple juice

- 1 egg, slightly beaten

- 1 c. Cool Whip

Directions

Add prepared Jell-O to 7-up and fruit. Transfer to a 9x13 inch dish to chill. Cook the sugar, flour, juice, and egg in a saucepan over medium heat. Thicken, and the cool down. Add cool whip. Spread mixture over Jell-O salad. Chill for 4 hours.

Lemon-Lime Whip Jell-O Salad

Ingredients

- 1 (3 oz.) package lemon Jell-O gelatin

- 1 (3 oz.) package lime Jell-O gelatin

- 2 c. boiling water

- 1 c. cold water

- 1 (20 oz.) can crushed pineapple, drained

- 1 c. Miracle Whip

- 1 tsp. horseradish

- 1 (24 oz.) carton cottage cheese

- 1 can sweetened condensed milk

Directions

Prepare Jell-O and chill until almost set. Add remaining ingredients and stir well, return to chill.

Raspberry Jell-O Ice Cream Salad

Ingredients

- 1 package raspberry Jell-O gelatin

- 1 c. hot water

- 1 c. vanilla ice cream

- 1 (9 oz.) can crushed pineapple, un-drained

- 1/2 c. chopped pecan nuts

- 1 medium banana, sliced

Directions

Dissolve Jell-O in hot water and add ice cream until Jell-O dissolves. Add bananas, pineapple, and nuts. Put in a 1 quart mold to chill.

Grandma's Green Jell-O Salad

Ingredients

- 1 can crushed pineapple (in juice, not syrup)

- 2 c. pineapple juice

- 2 packages lime Jell-O gelatin

- 1 package cream cheese (cut into small pieces)

- 6 square ice cubes (old fashioned ice tray kind)

- 1 c. chopped walnuts or pecans

- 1 1/2 c. finely shredded cabbage

- 1 (16 oz.) container Cool Whip

Directions

Drain the pineapple and reserve 2 c. juice. Add water as needed. Boil the juice and prepare jell using the juice instead of hot water. Stir till completely blended. Blend in the cream cheese pieces, pineapple, and 6 ice cubes. Stir till cubes melt. Cool in the freezer so that it reaches the consistency of syrup. Add nuts, shredded cabbage, and cool whip. Chill 2 to 3 hours more.

Cranberry and Port Jell-O Salad

Ingredients

- 1 (6 oz.) box raspberry Jell-O gelatin

- 2 c. boiling water

- 1 (20 oz.) can crushed pineapple, drained

- 15 oz. whole berry cranberry sauce

- 1/2 c. walnuts, chopped

- 1/3 c. port wine

Directions

Prepare Jell-O as directed and put in a glass serving bowl to chill. Add the remaining ingredients and chill until mixture sets.

Cranberry Jell-O Salad with Cream Cheese Topping

Ingredients

- 1 lb. fresh cranberries

- 1 (20 oz.) can crushed pineapple

- 1/2 c. walnut pieces (or amount as desired)

- 2 packages raspberry Jell-O gelatin

- 2 c. boiling water

- 1 c. cold water

- 1 3/4 c. sugar

- 2 (8 oz.) packages cream cheese

Directions

Blend cranberries in a blender until fine. Mix with 1 ¾ c. sugar. Set aside to dissolve the sugar.
Prepare Jell-O as directed and set aside to cool. Combine pineapple, cranberries, walnuts, and Jell-O. Stir. Transfer to a 9x13 inch dish. Chill until set. Blend cream cheese and reserved pineapple juice with a mixer until whipped. Cover top of cooled Jell-O with cream cheese mixture and chill again before serving.

Cherry Coke Jell-O Salad

Ingredients

- 1 can cherry pie filling
- 1/4 c. sugar
- 1/2 c. water
- 1 (6 oz.) package cherry Jell-O
- 1 (12 oz.) can Coke
- 1 can pineapple chunk, cut in half or pineapple tidbits

Directions

Bring pie filling, sugar, water, and juice from the pineapples to a boil. Add soda to Jell-O mix.
Reduce heat and simmer until no longer foamy. Combine with pineapple and chill until firm.

Nutty Jell-O Salad

Ingredients

- 2 (3 oz.) packages lime Jell-O gelatin

- 2 (3 oz.) packages lemon Jell-O gelatin

- 2 (3 oz.) packages cherry Jell-O

- 1 (8 oz.) package cream cheese, cubed

- 1 (8 oz.) can crushed pineapple, un-drained

- 1/4 c. chopped nuts

- 2 c. whipped topping

Directions

Prepare lime Jell-O as directed and pour into a 9x13 inch pan greased with non-stick spray. Chill until almost firm. Dissolve lemon Jell-O as directed, and add cream cheese until it becomes smooth. Add nuts and crushed pineapple. Blend cool whip with lemon Jell-O mixture and chill 1 hour. Repeat step two for cherry Jell-O and pour into lemon layer. Chill for 4 hours. Serve with cool whip.

Pineapple Lemon Jell-O Salad

Ingredients

- 1 (6 oz.) package lemon Jell-O gelatin
- 1 c. crushed pineapple (drain and save juice)
- 2 bananas, sliced
- 2 c. miniature marshmallows
- 2 eggs, beaten
- 2 tbsps. butter
- 1/2 c. sugar
- 1 c. pineapple juice
- 2 tbsps. flour
- 1 c. Cool Whip
- Grated cheese
- Chopped nuts

Directions

Add pineapple, banana, and marshmallows to prepared

lemon Jell-O. Put in a 9x13 inch glass pan. Chill for 2 hours. Mix the eggs, butter, flour, and sugar on top of a double boiler. Add the pineapple juice from cooking until it thickens. Cool to firm. Add cool whip and put on top of Jell-O. Sprinkle with cheese and nuts.

Lemon Jell-O Salad

Ingredients

- 1 package lime or lemon Jell-O gelatin, in

- 1 1/2 c. boiling water

- 1/2 c. mayonnaise

- 4 tbsps. prepared horseradish

- 1/4 tsp. salt

- 1/2 tsp. paprika

- 1/2 c. heavy cream, whipped

Directions

Prepare Jell-O as directed and chill. Add mayonnaise, salt, horseradish, paprika, and whipped cream. Mix well. Chill for 4 hours. Serve.

7-UP and Banana Jell-O Salad

Ingredients

- 1 (6 oz.) package orange-pineapple flavored gelatin or raspberry Jell-O gelatin

- 2 c. water, boiling

- 1 c. small marshmallow

- 2 c. 7-Up soda

- 2 bananas, mashed

- Nuts (my kids don't want) (optional)

- 1 (20 oz.) can crushed pineapple, drained (keep 1 C. of liquid)

TOPPING

- 1 egg, beaten

- 1 c. pineapple juice (from above)

- 1/2 c. sugar

- 2 tbsps. flour

- 8 oz. whipped topping (I use Cool Whip)

Directions

Prepare Jell-O as directed; add 7-up and marshmallow. Stir until melted. Chill. Take crushed pineapple and bananas to add to Jell-O. Put into a dish, and chill till firm. Cook flour, sugar, juice, and egg on medium heat in a pan. Cool. Add cool whip when cooled. Spread on Jell-O mixture.

Mandarin Orange Jell-O Salad

Ingredients

- 1 (6 oz.) package lemon Jell-O gelatin

- 2 (8-12 oz.) cans mandarin oranges, drained

- 12 oz. frozen orange juice concentrate

Directions

Prepare Jell-O as directed and add the can of orange juice. Stir in mandarin oranges. Chill for 4 hours.

Green Jell-O Salad

Ingredients

- 1 (6 oz.) package lime Jell-O gelatin

- 1 (16 oz.) container Cool Whip (or equivalent)

- 1 (15 oz.) can crushed pineapple, drained

- 1 1/2 c. mini marshmallows (to taste)

- 1 pint cottage cheese

- 1/2 c. chopped walnuts

Directions

Dissolve lime Jell-O as directed, and chill. Add remaining ingredients, and put in a mold. Chill for 4 to 5 hours. Remove from mold, and add cool whip to the top.

Orange Grapefruit Jell-O Salad

Ingredients

- 1 large grapefruit, peeled and sectioned

- 1 orange, peeled and sectioned

- 3/4-1 c. orange juice

- 1 (3 oz.) package lemon gelatin

- 1 c. boiling water

- 1/2 c. coarsely chopped pecans

Directions

Drain the citrus fruit sections, and save the juice. Mix orange juice with reserved juices until it makes 1 c. In boiling water, dissolve gelatin and then add juice. Chill. Add fruit and pecans. Chill into a square dish till set. Cut in squares to serve.

Creamy Jell-O Salad

Ingredients

- 1 (6 oz.) box lime Jell-O gelatin (or 2 3-oz boxes)
- 2 c. boiling water
- 1 1/4 c. cold water
- 1 (3 oz.) box instant lemon pudding
- 2 c. milk
- 2 c. diced apples, unpeeled for color
- 1/2 c. chopped walnuts

Directions

Prepare Jell-O in 2 c. of boiling water. Add 1 ¼ c. of cold water. Chill for 1 ½ hours to set.
Blend the lemon pudding with milk in a large bowl, according to directions. Chill for 5 minutes.
Mix the pudding with the Jell-O well. Beat for 2 minutes with a mixer. Add dice apples and walnuts. Chill in a 9x13 inch pan. Serve with Cool Whip on top.

Lemon/Lime Cream Cheese Jell-O Salad

Ingredients

- 1 (6 oz.) package lemon Jell-O gelatin or lime Jell-O gelatin

- 1 (8 oz.) package cream cheese (not fat free)

- 1/2 c. nuts

- 1 (11 oz.) can Sprite or 7-up or carbonated lemon-lime beverage

- 1 c. water, boiling

- 1 (6 oz.) can crushed pineapple, drained

Directions

Prepare the Jell-O in hot water. Add cream cheese till smooth. Mix in the pineapple and nuts. Blend in sprite. Pour into a mold to chill and set.

Blueberry Jell-O Salad

Ingredients

- 1 (6 oz.) box raspberry Jell-O gelatin
- 1 1/4 c. hot water
- 1 (15-20 oz.) can un-drained crushed pineapple
- 1 (16-21 oz.) can blueberry pie filling
- 8 oz. cream cheese
- 1 c. sugar
- 8 oz. sour cream

Directions

Dissolve Jell-O in water. Add pineapple and pie-filling, reserving 1/4 c. of pie-filling for garnish. Place Jell-O mixture in a large decorative glass bowl (one that holds about 6-8 c.) and chill until it sets up. Cream together cream cheese, sugar and sour cream. Spread on top of Jell-O and top with reserved 1/4 c. pie-filling in center of cream mixture for garnish. Refrigerate.

Jell-O Salad

Ingredients

- 1 lb. cottage cheese

- 1 (3 oz.) box any flavor Jell-O gelatin powder

- 1 c. whipped topping

- 1 (4 oz.) can crushed pineapple, well drained

Directions

Blend ingredients in the order listed, and chill for 2 hours.

Sugar-Free Jell-O Salad

Ingredients

- 1 (1/3 oz.) package sugar-free strawberry gelatin
- 1 c. boiling water
- 1 1/2 c. frozen unsweetened strawberries, thawed and halved
- Vegetable oil cooking spray
- 1 (1/3 oz.) package sugar-free lemon gelatin
- 1 c. boiling water
- 4 oz. Neufchatel cheese, softened
- 1 c. skim milk
- 1 (1/3 oz.) package sugar-free lime gelatin
- 1 c. boiling water
- 1 (20 oz.) can crushed pineapple with juice, undrained

Directions

Prepare Gelatin according to directions. Add

strawberries. Coat a mold with cooking spray. Chill covered for 1 hour. Prepare the lemon gelatin, and set aside. Mix Neufchatel cheese with an electric mixer till smooth. Add milk, and beat well. Mix lemon gelatin with cheese mixture, and continue to beat at low speed. Pour over strawberry layer in mold. Chill covered for 1 hour. Prepare lime gelatin. Chill. Add pineapple over lemon layer, and cover and chill 1 hour more.

Orange Jell-O Salad

Ingredients

- 1 (3 oz.) package orange Jell-O

- 1 c. boiling water

- 1 (11 oz.) can mandarin oranges, drained

- 1 (6 oz.) can crushed pineapple, drained

- 1 (12 oz.) container Cool Whip

- 1 c. miniature marshmallow

- 1/2 c. walnuts, chopped (optional)

Directions

In boiling water, dissolve the Jell-O. Add mandarin oranges, drains, and crushed pineapple. Mix all other ingredients in well. Chill overnight.

Layered Holiday Jell-O Salad

Ingredients

- 1 (6 oz.) package cranberry Jell-O gelatin or cherry gelatin

- 1 (16 oz.) can whole berry cranberry sauce

- 1 (6 oz.) package lime Jell-O gelatin

- 1 (20 oz.) can crushed pineapple, un-drained, divided

- 1 c. sour cream (8oz container)

- 1 (8 oz.) package cream cheese

- 2 c. boiling water, divided

Directions

Mix red Jell-O in 1 c. boiling water until it dissolves. Add half the pineapple, and all the cranberry sauce. Put in a 9x13 inch dish to chill. Mix sour cream and cream cheese. Layer over the Jell-O. In another bowl, mix boiling water with the green Jell-O to dissolve. Add the rest of the pineapple, and chill to set. Spread a cream cheese layer over the green Jell-O. Cover and chill overnight.

Easy Jell-O Salad

Ingredients

- 2 (3 1/2 oz.) boxes orange Jell-O

- 1 (16 oz.) container Cool Whip (or more, depending on how creamy you want it)

- 1/2-1 c. sour cream, to taste

- Mandarin orange, for garnish, on top

Directions

Blend together Cool Whip, Jell-O, and sour cream. Put into a dish, and top with fruit. Serve immediately or chilled.

Chicken Salad with Cranberry/Lemon Jell-O Topping

Ingredients

- 1 (7 g) envelope Knox gelatin
- 1/4 c. cold water
- 1/4 c. boiling water
- 2 c. cooked chicken, chopped
- 1 c. chopped celery
- 1 c. mayonnaise
- 2 tbsps. dried onion flakes or fresh onions
- 1 (3 oz.) box lemon Jell-O gelatin
- 3/4 c. boiling water
- 1 (15 oz.) can jellied cranberry sauce
- 1/4 c. orange juice

Directions

.

Mix 1 envelope of gelatin in ¼ c. cold water. Then add ¼ c. of boiling water, and stir until dissolved. Mix in the chicken, mayo, celery, and onion. Add to a square pan. Chill. Blend lemon Jell-O, boiling water, cranberry sauce, and orange juice. Add to chicken mixture, and chill overnight.

Very Berry Jell-O Salad

Ingredients

- 2 c. cranberry juice cocktail

- 1 (6 oz.) package red Jell-O

- 1 1/2 c. club soda

- 1/4 crème de cassis

- 1 tsp. fresh lemon juice

- 3 c. assorted blueberries or raspberries or sliced strawberries

Directions

Mix cranberry juice and gelatin together in a pot to boil for 2 minutes. Add club soda, liqueur, and lemon juice. Chill for 1 to ½ hours to thicken slightly. Add 2 c. of berries. Put in mold, and chill for 4 hours. Remove from mold, and top with 1 c. of berries.

Creamy Cucumber and Onion Jell-O Salad

Ingredients

- 1 (3 oz.) package lime Jell-O gelatin

- 1 tsp. salt

- 1 c. boiling water

- 2 tbsps. vinegar

- 1-2 tsp. grated onion

- 1 c. sour cream

- 1/2 c. mayonnaise (Hellman's is best for this)

- 2 c. diced cucumbers

Directions

Use salt water to dissolve Jell-O, while boiling. Mix in vinegar and onion. Chill to set. Transfer to a bowl. In a separate bowl, blend sour cream and mayonnaise. Add to Jell-O before it fully sets. Add cucumbers, and then chill to fully set.

Fruity Cottage Cheese Jell-O Salad

Ingredients

- 1 (12 oz.) carton cottage cheese

- 1 (3 oz.) package Jell-O gelatin (any flavor)

- 1 (8 oz.) can fruit cocktail (drained)

- Additional fruit, cut up (banana, apple, mandarin oranges) (optional)

- Mini marshmallows (optional)

- Cool Whip

Directions

Blend cottage cheese and Jell-O well. Mix in the drained fruit cocktail with additional fruit, and mini marshmallows. Top with cool whip and stir.

Marshmallow Jell-O Salad

Ingredients

- 1 (3 oz.) box lime Jell-O gelatin
- 1 (3 oz.) box lemon Jell-O gelatin
- 1/2 pint whipping cream
- 8 oz. cream cheese
- 1 c. miniature marshmallow
- 1 (8 oz.) can crushed pineapple, drained

Directions

Prepare each Jell-O mix separately. Whip the cream so that it peaks. Blend small chunks of cream cheese in so that it is thick and chunky. Fold pineapple, marshmallows, and Jell-O flavors together. Add to a large bowl, and chill overnight while covered.

Pineapple Cottage Cheese Jell-O Salad

Ingredients

- 2 (3 oz.) packages lime Jell-O gelatin

- 1 lb. cottage cheese

- 1 (6 oz.) can crushed pineapple, drained. If desired, a little bit of this liquid can be put into the Jell-O mix.

- 2 tbsps. mayonnaise

- 1 tbsp. apple cider vinegar

Directions

Prepare Jell-O according to directions, and use 2 tbsps. less water. Mix in the mayonnaise and vinegar well. Chill in a covered dish. Add cottage cheese, and pineapple when it begins to set.

Pineapple Whip Jell-O Salad

Ingredients

- 1 (3 oz.) box lemon Jell-O gelatin

- 1 (3 oz.) box lime Jell-O gelatin

- 2 c. boiling water

- 1 quart small curd cottage cheese (the large one)

- 1 (20 oz.) can crushed pineapple in syrup

- 1 c. Miracle Whip

Directions

Prepare Jell-O according to package. Mix in Miracle Whip until smooth. Blend in cottage cheese and pineapple with its syrup. Chill to set.

Pineapple Pecan Jell-O Salad

Ingredients

- 1 (3 oz.) package lime Jell-O gelatin

- 1 (3 oz.) package lemon Jell-O gelatin

- 1 c. boiling water

- 1 (20 oz.) can pineapple tidbits (drain well)

- 1 pint cottage cheese (2 c.)

- 1 tbsp. horseradish

- 1 c. walnuts or pecans (chopped)

- 1 c. mayonnaise

- 1 c. heavy whipping cream (whipped)

Directions

Prepare the Jell-O in boiling water. Set aside cottage cheese and whipped cream. Blend remaining ingredients. Cool and add cottage cheese and whipped cream. Chill to mold in a 9x13 inch dish.

Lemon Jell-O Salad

Ingredients

- 2 (1/3 oz.) packages Jell-O sugar-free lemon gelatin

- 2 (3 1/2 oz.) packages Jell-O instant lemon pudding

- 2 (16 oz.) cans crushed pineapple with juice

- 2 c. miniature marshmallows

- 4 c. Cool Whip

Directions

Prepare Jell-O according to directions, and add instant pudding, pineapple, and juice. Mix in marshmallows and Cool whip.

DISCLAIMER AND/OR LEGAL NOTICES: Every effort has been made to accurately represent this book and it's potential. Results vary with every individual, and your results may or may not be different from those depicted. No promises, guarantees or warranties, whether stated or implied, have been made that you will produce any specific result from this book. Your efforts are individual and unique, and may vary from those shown. Your success depends on your efforts, background and motivation.

The material in this publication is provided for educational and informational purposes only and is not intended as medical advice. The information contained in this book should not be used to diagnose or treat any illness, metabolic disorder, disease or health problem. Always consult your physician or health care provider before beginning any nutrition or exercise program. Use of the programs, advice, and information contained in this book is at the sole choice and risk of the readers.